Let's Play Cards

Authors

John Belton
Joella Cramblit

 RAINTREE EDITIONS

2☐3☐4☐5☐6☐7☐8☐9☐0☐ 80☐79☐78☐77☐76☐

Published by   **Raintree Editions**
A Division of Raintree Publishers Limited.
Milwaukee, Wisconsin 53203

Distributed by   **Childrens Press**
1224 West Van Buren Street
Chicago, Illinois 60607

Library of Congress Cataloging in Publication Data

Belton, John, 1931-
   Let's play cards.

     SUMMARY: An illustrated introduction to cards
with instructions for five simple games and a glossary
of basic terms.
     1. Cards—Juvenile Literature. (1. Cards. 2. Games)
I. Cramblit, Joella, joint author.
II. Title.
GV1244.B44 795.4 75-9606
ISBN 0-8172-0026-6
ISBN 0-8172-0025-8 lib. bdg.

Contents

1
Learning About Cards

A **deck** of cards is made up of rectangular-shaped pieces of thick, stiff paper with numbers and pictures. They are used for playing games.

Most decks have fifty-two cards, but there are many more than fifty-two games you can play with a deck of cards.

A deck of cards has four **suits**: two red suits and two black suits.

The two red suits are diamonds and hearts.

The two black suits are clubs and spades.

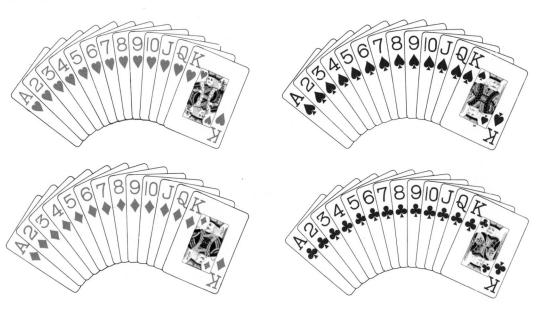

This is what a heart looks like.

This is what a spade looks like.

This is what a diamond looks like.

This is what a club looks like.

Each suit has thirteen cards.

There are ten **number cards** and three **face cards.**

Sometimes the number cards are called spot cards. The spots are either diamonds, hearts, clubs, or spades.

Notice how each card has a number in two corners. Notice how each card is covered with small hearts. The **Ace** is number 1 and the other cards are numbered from 2 to 10.

Count only the small hearts. Notice how the number of small hearts on each card equal the number in the corner of each card.

There are three face cards.
Sometimes the face cards
are called picture cards
because there is a picture of
a face on each card.
Sometimes the face cards
are also called high cards.

Notice how each card has a
letter in two corners and a
face on both ends.

The J card is called a Jack.

The Q card is called a
Queen.

The K card is called a King.

The Jack is the card that
comes after the 10. It is
higher in value, which
means it is worth more.
Think of the Jack as an 11.

The Queen is the card that
comes after the Jack.

The King is the card that
comes after the Queen.

The King is the highest
card.

J ♥

9

Notice we have told you about the cards from the lowest card (Ace) to the highest card (King).

But in some games you will play, the Ace is the highest card. When this happens, the 2 is the lowest card instead of the Ace.

Now look at your deck of cards. Find the number cards and the face cards in all the suits.

Now it's time to learn what to do with a deck of cards.

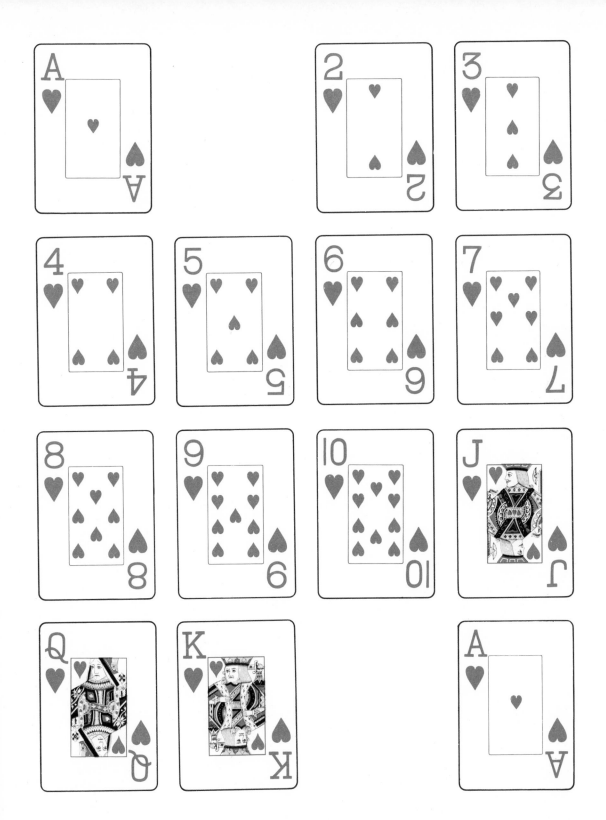

2
Card Talk

Before you play a game of cards, you must get the cards ready for a game. You do this by **shuffling, dealing, fanning,** and **sorting** the cards.

Shuffling the cards

To shuffle means to mix the pack of cards so the same suits and same numbers are not together.

This is how you shuffle.

1 Place the cards face down in front of you. Face down means you cannot see the numbers and pictures on the cards. You see only the design that is on the back side of the cards.

2 Divide the cards into two piles.

14

3 Put the piles at an angle so the tips touch and overlap a little.

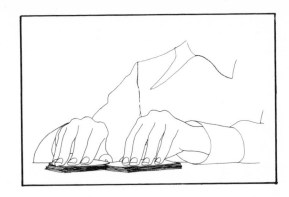

4 Place your thumbs along the inside of the cards and your fingers on top of the cards.

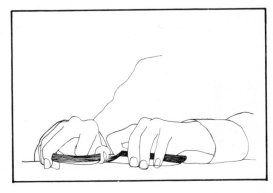

5 With your thumbs, pull the cards up on the inside and bend them a little. With your fingers, hold the cards down on top. Push your fingertips down.

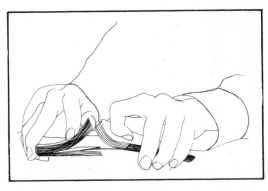

6 Let the cards drop slowly, first from one pile, then the other. Do this by moving up the tips of your thumbs. But, remember—hold the cards down with your fingers!

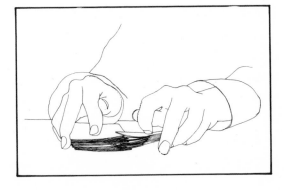

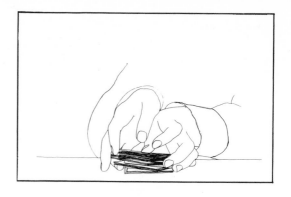

7 When all the cards have dropped, push them together.

8 Repeat until the cards are well mixed.

Anyone can shuffle the cards for a game, so go over these steps and practice until you can shuffle well. You should always shuffle the cards before a new game.

Dealing the cards

To deal means to hand out the cards to the players. The person who hands out the cards for a game is called the **dealer.**

To choose a dealer, spread the deck of cards face down. Each player picks one card. The player with the highest card is the dealer. The Ace is high card. If two or more players pick the same high card, both pick a new card. If you play the *same* game again, the player on the left becomes the new dealer.

This is how you deal.

1 First, hold the deck of cards—face down—in one hand. With your other hand, take one card from the top of the deck. Give the first card to the player on your left.

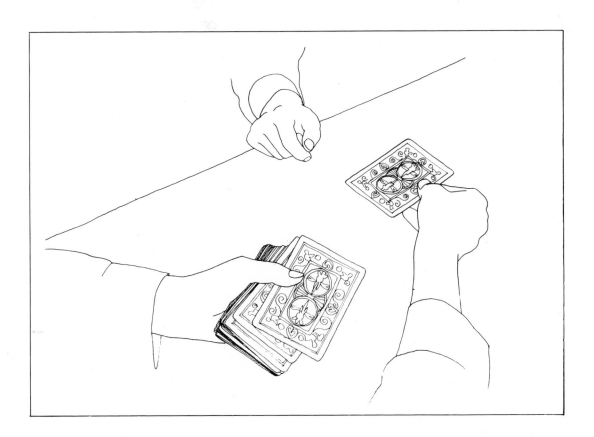

2 Continue around the table. Deal one card at a time to each player, always ending with dealer. The dealer stops dealing when each player has the number of cards needed for the game to be played.

3 Some card games use all the cards. It might happen that one or two players will get more cards than another player. This is all right because all the cards must be used.

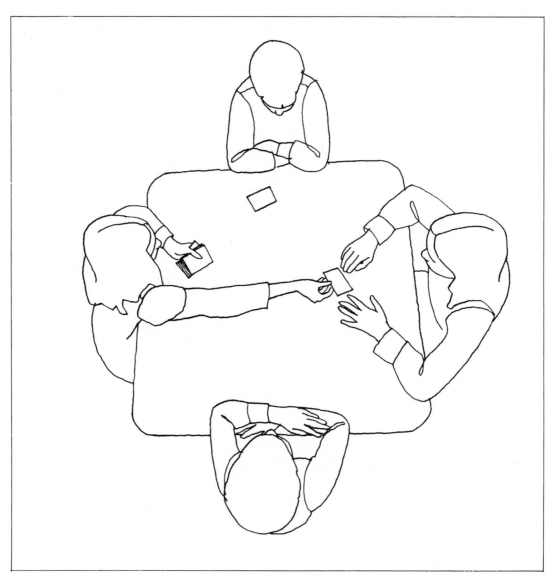

Fanning the cards

To fan your cards means to hold your cards a certain way in your hand.

This is how you fan your cards.

1 Hold the cards in one hand. With your other hand, spread out the top of the cards like a fan. This uncovers the corner of each card.

2 Now you can see all your cards but no one else can.

Sorting your cards

To sort your cards means to put next to each other the cards that have the same number, face, or suit. You can have pairs, three of a kind, four of a kind, or suits depending on the game you play.

This is how you sort your cards.

1 Put your pairs together. A pair is two cards with the same number or picture.

Two 5's are a pair and two Kings are a pair.

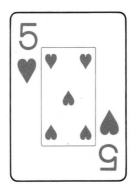 

2 Put three of a kind
together. Three of a kind
are three cards with the
same number or picture.
Three 6's are three of a kind
and three Queens are three
of a kind.

3 Put four of a kind
together. Four of a kind are
four cards with the same
number or picture. Four 7's
are four of a kind and four
Jacks are four of a kind.

4 Put all your suits together. Suits are diamonds, hearts, clubs, and spades. If you have two spades, two diamonds, one heart, and one club, you put the suits together.

Now you know how to sort your cards. But the *way* you sort your cards depends on the game you play.

Playing cards will be more fun if you follow these rules:

1 Hold your cards so no one else can see them.

2 Never look at another player's cards.

3 Wait your turn before you play.

Now, let's play cards.

3
Old Maid

Players ———————————— Two or more

Object of Game ————— To match your cards in pairs and not be the one holding the Old Maid at the end of the game

Before Shuffling ———— Remove the Queen of Hearts, the Queen of Diamonds, and the Queen of Spades from the deck of cards. You will not play with these three Queens. You will play with the Queen of Clubs. The Queen of Clubs is the Old Maid.

Deal ————————————— Deal out all the cards, one at a time, to the players. Some players may get an extra card. If there are four players, each player gets twelve cards except Player 1, who will get thirteen cards.

Q
♣

♣
Q

This Is How You Play Old Maid.

1 Sort your cards in pairs, if you have any. Take out all the pairs you are holding. Put them face down in a pile in front of you. You play with the cards left in your hand.

2 After you have removed your pairs, fan your cards.

3 The dealer starts this game by taking the first turn. Dealer picks one card from the hand of the player on the left (or Player 1).

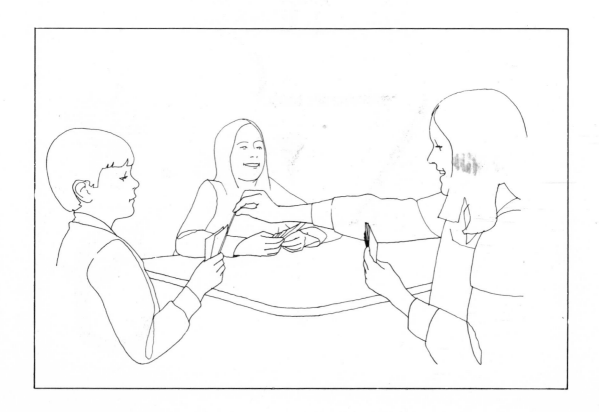

4 If the card picked matches one the dealer has, this is a pair. She shows the pair to the other players. Then she puts the pair face down on the pile in front of her. If the card does not match one she has, she adds that card to the cards in her hand. She does not show it to the other players. This ends the dealer's turn.

5 Player 1 now picks a card from the player on his left (Player 2). After he picks a card, he follows Step 4.

6 Play continues around the table. Each player picks a card from the player on his left when it is his turn.

Dealer picks from Player 1; Player 1 picks from Player 2; Player 2 picks from Player 3; Player 3 picks from Dealer.

7 The game is over when all the cards are paired and one player is left with the Queen of Clubs.

8 The player left holding the Old Maid loses the game.

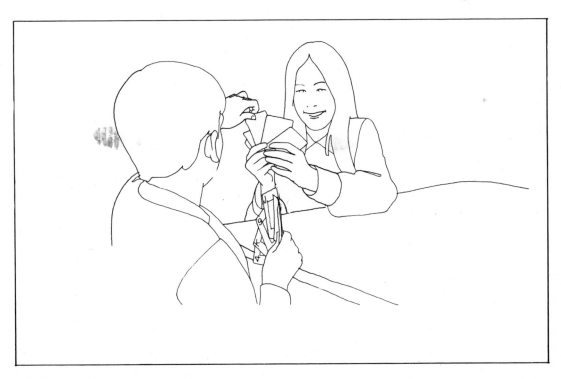

4
Go Fish

Players ——————————— Two to eight

Object of Game ——————— To be the player to collect the most sets of four of a kind

Deal ——————————————— If there are two players, deal out seven cards, one at a time. If there are more than two players, deal out five cards, one at a time.

The cards that are not dealt out are spread out, face down, in the middle of the table. This is the Fish pile.

This Is How You Play Go Fish.

Dealer

1 Fan your cards. Sort your cards. Put the same numbers and pictures next to each other.

2 The dealer starts this game. He asks *any* player for a card to match a card he is already holding in his hand.

Player 1

3 For example, the dealer will ask Player 2, ''Do you have any 4's?''

4 Player 2 gives the dealer his 4.

5 Dealer asks Player 1, ''Do you have any 4's?''

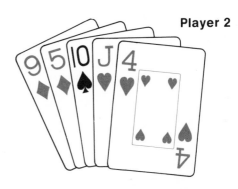

Player 2

6 Player 1 does not have any 4's. Player 1 says ''Go Fish.''

7 The dealer picks one card from the Fish pile in the middle of the table. The dealer is lucky! He picked up a 4, the same number card he wanted. He shows the 4 to the other players.

Player 3

8 Because the dealer picked the card he wanted, he gets another turn. Again, he may ask any player for any card to match one he is holding in his hand.

Dealer

The dealer now has three 4's. If he gets one more 4 he will have a set of four of a kind.

Player 1

9 Dealer asks Player 3, "Do you have any 4's?"

10 Player 3 does not have a 4. Player 3 says, "Go Fish."

Player 2

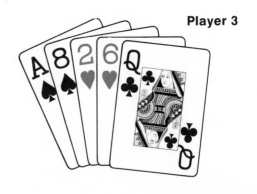

Player 3

11 The dealer does not pick up a 4 from the Fish pile. Because he did not pick a 4, he does not show the card to the other players.

12 The dealer's turn is now over because he did not get the card he asked for from Player 3 or from the Fish pile.

13 Now it is Player 1's turn. Player 1 follows the same steps the dealer followed.

14 The playing continues around the table with each player taking his turn until all the cards are collected into sets of four by the players.

15 When a player gets four of a kind, he shows them to the other players. After showing the set of four, the player puts them face down in front of him.

16 If a player runs out of cards before the Fish pile is gone, he picks five cards from the Fish pile. He continues to play.

17 The game ends when all the players are out of cards and the Fish pile is gone.

18 The winner of Go Fish is the player who has the most sets of four of a kind.

5
War

Players	————————	Two to eight
Object of Game	—————	To win all the cards
Deal	———————	Deal out all the cards, one at a time, to the players. Some players may get an extra card.

This Is How You Play War.

1 Put your cards, face down, in a pile in front of you.

2 Each player turns up one card.

3 The player with the highest card wins all the other cards. In this game the Ace is the highest card.

Player 2 won the three other cards because the Ace is higher than the Queen, 9, or 2.

Player 2 puts these four cards, face down, on the bottom of his pile.

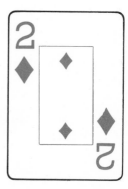

4 Sometimes, more than one player will turn up a card with the same number or picture. If the two cards that are the same are higher than the other cards turned up, there will be a War. The War will decide who will win the cards.

The Jack is higher than the two 9's.

The dealer's Jack wins the other three cards.

The two Aces are higher
than the 10 and 5.

The Aces will have a War.

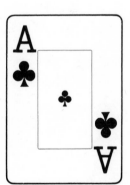

5 This is how you have a War.

Only Players 1 and 3 will have a War because they have both turned up an Ace. Players 1 and 3 take the top card from their pile and put it face down in front of them. The players do not look at the card they picked. Each player picks a second card from his pile, turns it

up, and puts it on top of the face-down card.

Player 3 turns up a Jack and Player 1 turns up an 8. Player 3 wins the war because the Jack is higher than the 8. Player 3 also wins Player 1's face-down card plus the 5 and 10 turned up by the Dealer and Player 2.

6 Play continues with each player turning up cards one at a time. The highest card always takes the other cards.

7 The game is over when one of the players wins all the cards.

8 The winner is the player who wins all fifty-two cards.

6
Slapjack

Players ——————————— Two to eight

Object of Game ————— To win all fifty-two cards

Deal ————————————— Deal out all the cards, one at a time. Some players may get an extra card.

This Is How You Play Slapjack.

1 Each player puts his cards face down in a pile in front of him.

2 The dealer starts the game. The dealer turns over his top card and puts this card in the middle of the table.

3 Player 1, the player to the left of the dealer, turns over his top card. He puts it on top of the card already in the middle of the table.

4 Each player takes a turn and makes sure to turn over his card quickly. Everyone should see the card at the same time. It isn't fair for one player to see the card before the other players.

5 Take turns going around the table, each player turning over a card.

6 Watch for a Jack to be turned. It can be any of the four Jacks.

7 When a Jack is turned, try to be the first one to slap the Jack with your hand.

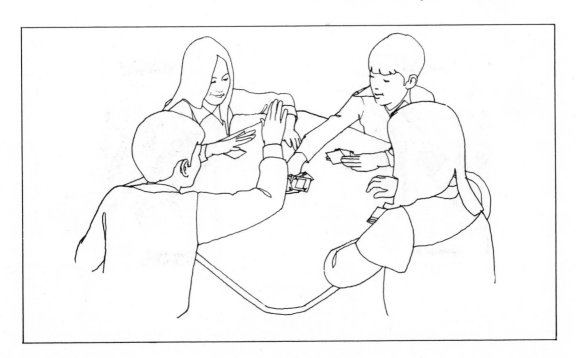

8 The first player to slap the Jack wins all the cards in the middle of the table. He puts these cards face down on the bottom of his own pile of cards.

9 The player on the left of the player who slapped the Jack starts a new pile in the middle of the table. He turns a card from his pile and puts it in the middle of the table.

10 The playing continues around the table with each player taking his turn. When a Jack is turned, the first player slapping the Jack again wins the pile of cards. He puts them, face down, on the bottom of his pile of cards.

11 The player to the left of the Jack-slapper begins the game again.

12 The quicker each player takes his turn and turns his card, the more exciting the game.

13 If a player loses all his cards, he stays in the game until the next Jack is turned. If he slaps the Jack first, he wins the cards in the middle of the table and stays in the game. If he does not slap the Jack first, he is out of the game because he is out of cards.

14 It is not fair to use one hand for turning cards and the other hand for slapping. You must use the same hand for turning and slapping.

15 It is not fair to slap a card that is not a Jack. If you slap the wrong card, you must give the player who played the card you slapped one card from your own pile. Pass it to him face down.

16 The game is over when one player wins all fifty-two cards.

17 The winner is the player who wins the fifty-two cards.

7
Pig

Players ———————	Three to thirteen
Object of Game —————	Not to be the last player to put his finger on his nose after a player has four of a kind
Before Shuffling —————	Remove from the deck one set of four of a kind for each player. You will not play with the rest of the deck.
	If there are four players, you will play with four sets of four of a kind, or sixteen cards. If there are five players, you will play with five sets of four of a kind, or twenty cards. Always add one more set of four of a kind for each extra player.
Deal ————————	Deal four cards to each player, one at a time.

This Is How You Play Pig.

1 When you play this game, you must remember to keep your eye on the other players. Watch for a player to put his finger on his nose. When a player does this, you quickly put your finger on your nose also, but you don't tell anyone.

2 Fan your cards. Put your cards that match next to each other.

3 Each player picks out one card he does not want.

4 At the same time, all the players put the card they do not want face down on the table. Each player then passes his card to the player on his left. All players pass the cards at the same time.

5 Each player picks up the card that is passed to him and looks at the card. Does it match a card already in the hand? If it does, put it next to the card it matches.

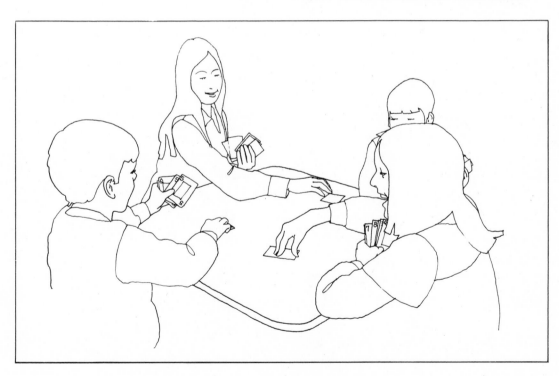

6 Wait until all the players have looked at their cards. When all the players are ready, each player picks another card he does not want. Again he passes the card to the player on his left. All players pass the cards at the same time.

7 Continue to pass cards at the same time to the player on the left, until one player gets four of a kind.

8 As soon as a player gets four of a kind, he puts his finger on his nose. Don't tell anyone if you have four of a kind or if you see a player put his finger on his nose. There will be one player who will be the last one to notice.

9 The last one to put his finger on his nose is the PIG and loses the game.

Glossary

Ace
A card that can be high or low, depending on the game being played. When the Ace is low, it counts as 1 and comes before the 2. When the Ace is high, it follows the King.

Dealer
Person who gives out the cards to each player.

Dealing
Handing out the cards to the players.

Deck
A pack of fifty-two cards.

Face Cards
The Jacks, Queens, and Kings of any suit. Face cards are also called picture cards or high cards.

Fanning
Spreading out the cards in
your hand, so just the
corners of each card show.

Number Cards
Any cards starting with the
Ace (Number 1) and
numbered from 2 up to 10.
Number cards are also
called spot cards.

Shuffling
Mixing the pack of cards
before dealing.

Sorting
Putting together cards that
are a pair, three of a kind,
four of a kind, or the same
suit.

Suits
Hearts, Spades, Diamonds
or Clubs. Each suit has
thirteen cards.

Design   Interface Design Group